CONTENTS

D1532704

THE GOSPEL
GOD'S PLAN FOR ME

gos·pel—noun. good news. The message about Christ, the kingdom of God, and salvation

GOD RULES.
The Bible tells us God created everyting, including you and me, and He is in charge of everything. *Genesis 1:1; Revelation 4:11; Colossians 1:16-17*

WE SINNED.
We all choose to disobey God. The Bible calls this sin. Sin separates us from God and deserves God's punishment of death. *Romans 3:23; 6:23*

GOD PROVIDED.
God sent Jesus, the perfect solution to our sin problem, to rescue us from the punishment we deserve. It's something we, as sinners, could never earn on our own. Jesus alone saves us. *John 3:16; Ephesians 2:8-9*

JESUS GIVES.
He lived a perfect life, died on the cross for our sins, and rose again. Because Jesus gave up His life for us, we can be welcomed into God's family for eternity. This is the best gift ever! *Romans 5:8; 2 Corinthians 5:21; 1 Peter 3:18; Ephesians 2:8-9*

WE RESPOND.
Believe in your heart that Jesus alone saves you through what He's already done on the cross. Repent, turning from self and sin to Jesus. Tell God and others that your faith is in Jesus. *John 14:6; Romans 10:9-10, 13*

UNEXPECTED SALVATION

In the story of Gideon, God used some unexpected weapons to save His people: jars, torches, and trumpets. In the New Testament, God also saved His people in an unexpected way by sending Jesus to die on a cross for sins. In both stories, God did what was impossible for man. Look up the verse listed above and write it in the space provided.

Book   **Chapter**   **Verse**

_____

_____

_____

_____

_____

BAD HABIT GOOD HABIT

In the book of Judges, the Israelites fell into the habit of rejecting the Lord. Each time, God sent a judge to save them. Jesus is the ultimate judge and Savior who rescues people from sin. Christians should be in the habit of sharing Jesus' gospel with everyone they know. On the chart below, write the names of five people you can share the gospel with.

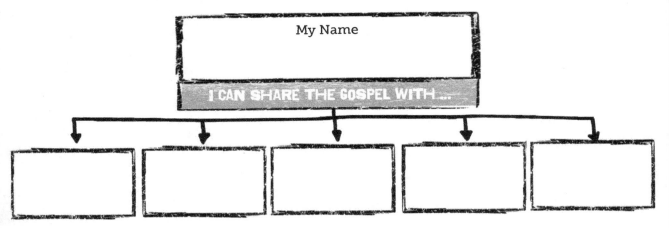

My Name

I CAN SHARE THE GOSPEL WITH ...

THAT'S IMPOSSIBLE!! (NOT WITH GOD!!)

In the space below, write down or draw all the Bible stories you can think of when God did something that was impossible for man to do. We've listed a few to get you started.

- **God created the world**

- **God delivered his people from egypt**

REBUILD THE PUZZLE

Fill the empty puzzle pieces with the words from the matching pieces below to complete part of today's memory verse.

L SE

THE OR IFY

H GLO OU

THE R D OF

NOTHING TOO BROKEN

Just like He restored the temple, God can restore anything that is broken in your life too! Draw a picture of something broken and then a picture of the the broken things after it is fixed.

Write down some broken things that you can ask God to rebuild and restore. This can be anything you are worried about or feel sad about.

MEETING 17

GOD'S PEOPLE WORK TOGETHER ON MISSION

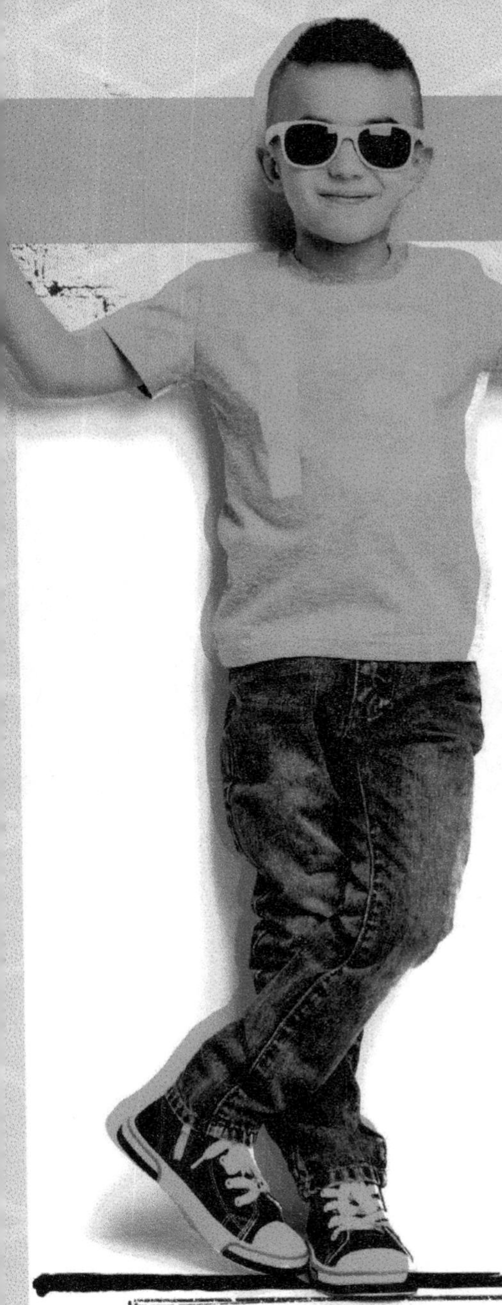

BUILD-A- VERSE

Nehemiah and the people worked hard to rebuild the wall around Jerusalem. Using today's memory verse, number the bricks in order of how they fit into the verse.

1 WHENEVER YOU

4 RALLY TO US THERE.

5 OUR GOD WILL

2 HEAR THE

3 TRUMPET SOUND,

6 FIGHT FOR US!!

1

2

3

4

5

6

SCRAMBLE CODE

Solve the code to discover the right letters, then unscramble the words to find out what God wants Christians to do!

H = <3   T = (pencil)   G = (megaphone)   W = (globe)

E = (microphone)   R = (book)   K = (alarm clock)   O = (phone)

☐ ☐ ☐ ☐ ➡ ☐ ☐ ☐ ☐

☐ ☐ ☐ ☐ ☐ ☐ ☐ ☐ ➡ ☐ ☐ ☐ ☐ ☐ ☐ ☐ ☐ ☐ ☐

TRACE IT

Trace the different lines to discover people you can tell about Jesus.

A-MAZE-ING

Find your way through the maze. Pick up the letters you find along the way to find out one job Christians are given. We are sent to be ...

START

FINISH

CRUNCH THE NUMBERS

LOCATE THE 23RD BOOK OF THE OLD TESTAMENT. WRITE IT HERE:

$3 + 50 =$ WRITE THE ANSWER HERE TO REVEAL THE CHAPTER NUMBER:

$7 - 2 =$ WRITE THE ANSWER HERE TO REVEAL THE VERSE NUMBER:

Look up the memory verse to discover what Isaiah prophesied about Jesus 700 years before His birth!

GOSPEL TRUTH

Jesus wants you to share His gospel with everyone! Reverse the letters in each word below to reveal gospel truths you can share from Isaiah 53.

JESUS WAS...

DESIPSED

DEHSINUP

DEDNUOW

BELIEVERS RECEIVE...

ECAEP

GNILAEH

SSENSUOETHGIR

Who's one person you know who needs to hear the gospel? Write their name here and say a prayer for them: _____

KNOWING WHAT'S AHEAD

Without flipping forward any pages in your activity book, take your best guess at the following questions:

» **HOW MANY PAGES ARE IN THIS ACTIVITY BOOK?**

» **DOES THE 1ST WORD ON PAGE 74 START WITH A CONSONANT OR A VOWEL?**

» **WHAT COLOR MAKES UP THE BACKGROUND OF PAGE 69?**

» **WHAT'S THE LAST NUMBER ON THE BARCODE WRITTEN ON THE BACK COVER OF THIS BOOK?**

» **NOW USE YOUR ACTIVITY BOOK TO DISCOVER HOW MANY QUESTIONS YOU GOT RIGHT.**

Humans don't even know what lies ahead in a simple activity book, but God knows everything before it happens. Turn to Isaiah 53 and list some things the prophet wrote about Jesus more than 700 years before He was even born!

CLEAN HEARTS

Cross out each black heart and write the remaining words in the space below to discover what can happen when you live on mission by sharing the gospel.

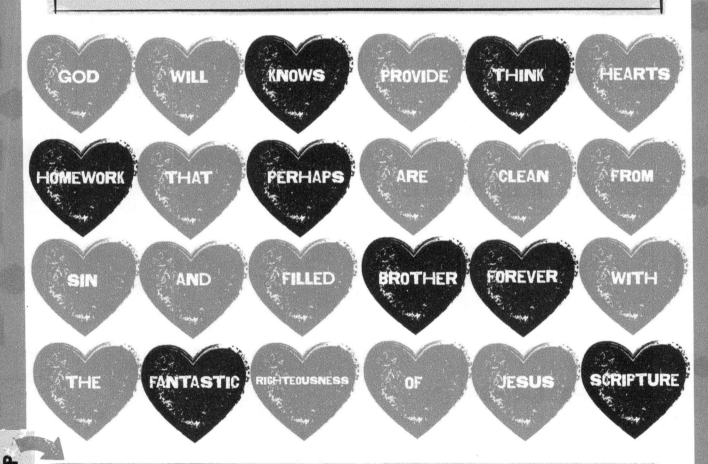

FRIEND FLIP

The previous puzzle relates to the verse from today's story, Jeremiah 31:33. Pair up with a friend and take turns tossing a coin onto the hearts above. If the coin covers mostly a pink heart, practice looking up and saying Jeremiah 31:33. If the coin covers mostly a black heart, share a person in your life who needs to hear about Jesus. Pray together for that person.

OBJECT LESSONS

Jeremiah used a tree branch, a hammer, and a cup to illustrate that God must judge sin. Unscramble and insert the words which are attached to correct puzzle pieces to reveal an exciting truth hinted about in Jeremiah 31!

TIHER PCALE

FGOIRVE SNRIENS

JEDGUD GITULY

GOD CAN

BECAUSE JESUS WAS

ON THE CROSS IN

SHEPHERD'S TO-DO LIST

Draw lines between the sheep descriptions on the left and what the True Shepherd, Jesus, will do for each on the right.

SHEEP ARE:	JESUS WILL:
WEAK	GIVE REST
INJURED	RESCUE
LOST	BIND UP/HEAL
HUNGRY	STRENGTHEN
IN DANGER	SEARCH FOR
AFRAID	FEED

Hold your pointer finger a few inches above the lists. Close your eyes and bring your finger down. What word pair are you touching? Use the space below to write out how Jesus accomplishes that shepherding work through the cross.

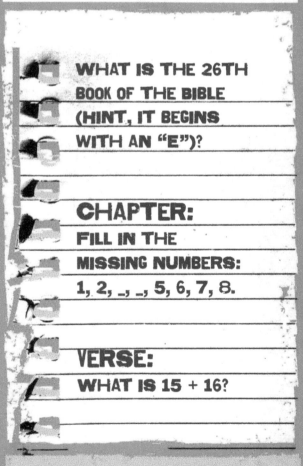

SCATTERED CLUES

Answer the questions using your Bible and these three clues to discover today's memory verse.

WHAT IS THE 26TH BOOK OF THE BIBLE (HINT, IT BEGINS WITH AN "E")?

CHAPTER:
FILL IN THE MISSING NUMBERS:
1, 2, _, _, 5, 6, 7, 8.

VERSE:
WHAT IS 15 + 16?

Look up this verse in your Bible. How would this have been encouraging news to God's people who were exiled (or scattered) in different places?

ACROSS THE WORLD

God is gathering people to His kingdom just as a shepherd gathers lost sheep. Christians from many nations make up the flock of God.

Circle the places below where God might have lost sheep. (Careful, some of these are made up!) When you're done, flip the page over and read the words at the bottom to see how many you got right.

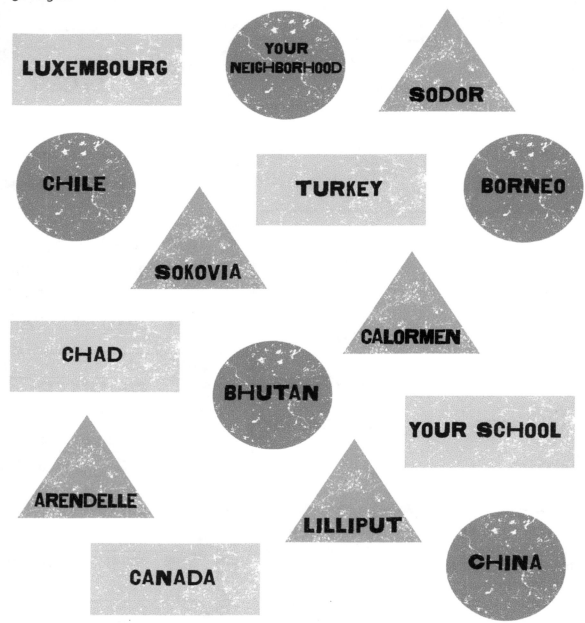

Only the words in triangles were made up places. The rest are real places to take the gospel
What role can you play in taking the gospel to some of these places? China, your
neighborhood, Chile, Borneo, Bhutan, Luxembourg, your school, Chad, Turkey, Canada

EXILE ADVICE

Cross out the second letter of this chain and then every other letter that follows. (We've started it for you!) Write down the remaining letters in order in the space below to reveal an important truth from this week's memory verse (1 Peter 2:11).

ARSGTVEBMNPMOQRWAERTYU ROEPSAISDFEGNHTJSK OLFK TLHMINSB WVOCRXIZDW, KSERETPY FHRJOKML SWICN.

EXTRA CREDIT: How did Shadrach, Meshach, and Abednego model this truth in today's story from the book of Daniel?

THIS OR THAT?

Circle the correct word or phrase in each sentence. Look up Daniel 3 and today's memory verse in 1 Peter 2:11 if you're not sure of an answer.

➤➤ KING NEBUCHADNEZZAR TOLD PEOPLE TO DANCE/BOW DOWN TO HIS STATUE WHEN THEY HEARD THE MUSIC.

➤➤ SHADRACH, MESHACH, AND ABEDNEGO OBEYED/REFUSED TO FOLLOW THE KING'S RULE.

➤➤ THE THREE FRIENDS DOUBTED/TRUSTED THAT GOD COULD SAVE THEM.

➤➤ THE KING HAD THE THREE FRIENDS THROWN INTO A TRASH COMPACTOR/A FURNACE.

➤➤ A FOURTH/FIFTH PERSON, EITHER AN ANGEL OR GOD HIMSELF, APPEARED IN THE FURNACE WITH THE THREE FRIENDS.

➤➤ GOD REVEALED HIS POWER BY RENAMING/SAVING THE THREE FRIENDS.

➤➤ THE THREE FRIENDS WERE EXILES/AT HOME IN BABYLON.

➤➤ CHRISTIANS ARE TO THINK OF THEMSELVES AS STRANGERS/CITIZENS OF THIS WORLD. THEIR REAL HOME IS IN NORTH AMERICA/HEAVEN.

DRAWING THE GOSPEL

Christians are called to live as faithful exiles (or strangers) in the world. Like Shadrach, Meshach, and Abednego, believers should look different from unbelievers but should also work for the good of those around them. The primary way Christians do this is by sharing the gospel and living it out in their communities. In the space below, finish drawing pictures that represent the gospel. Make your own gospel drawing in the last space.

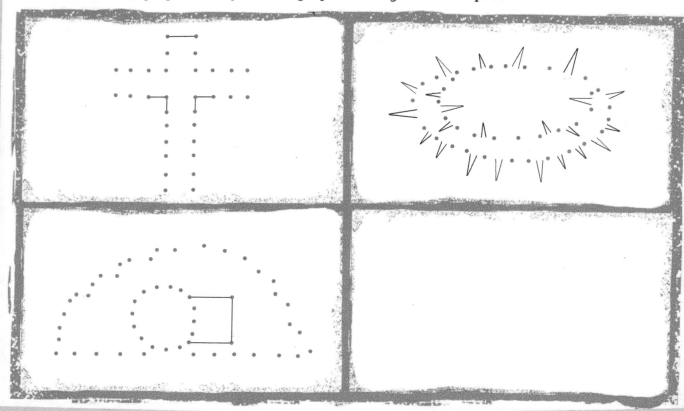

SUMMING IT UP

Add the bottom two numbers in each pyramid and write the answer in the top circle. Match that number's corresponding letter in the puzzle below to reveal an important message from today's memory verse in Jonah 4:2.

	4 3	7 6	2 8	3 3	5 3
	E	Y	M	C	R

JONAH IS A BOOK ABOUT GOD'S GREAT

◯ ◯ ◯ ◯ ◯ !
10 7 8 6 13

REACHING THE NATIONS

Jonah was the only prophet in the Old Testament who was sent to preach to a foreign nation on its own soil. Today, Jesus calls believers to take the message of the gospel to people all over the world. Circle the symbols that represent different ways Christians can share the gospel.

Pick one of the ways to share the gospel you may not have thought of before. Write an example of how you could tell others about Jesus in this way.

_____
_____
_____
_____
_____
_____
_____
_____

MERCIFUL CHOICES

Circle the correct answers. Then, unscramble the letters next to the correct answers to complete the sentence at the bottom:

God used which living thing to teach Jonah?

» A FISH (M)
» A VINE (B)
» A WORM (T)
» ALL OF THE ABOVE (O)

God rebuked Jonah for caring more about a plant than thousands of _____ in Nineveh?

» PEOPLE (L)
» SCROLLS (H)
» PIZZAS (R)
» BIRDS (G)

God showed the Ninevities mercy because they _____.

» READ THE BIBLE (U)
» GAVE JONAH MONEY (Y)
» RECYCLED (D)
» BELIEVED AND REPENTED (S)

God can show sinners mercy because _____.

» SIN ISN'T REALLY A BIG DEAL (C)
» GOD DOESN'T CARE ABOUT JUSTICE (I)
» LOVE IS ALL THAT MATTERS (W)
» JESUS WAS CRUCIFIED IN THEIR PLACE (A)

IF GOD SHOWS ME MERCY, I SHOULD SHOW MERCY TO OTHERS ___ ___ ___ ___ ___ .

CLEAR A PATH FOR THE KING

This week's memory verse, Malachi 3:1a, speaks of a messenger who would clear the way for Jesus. This was John the Baptist. Clear the path below by matching the letters to their corresponding rock outlines in the question below.

Extra credit: How does this act prepare hearts for Jesus?

T
B
N
C
E
A
P
R
E
L
I

Both John and Malachi told people to:

_____ _____ _____ _____ _____ _____

POINTING TO CHRIST

Every book in the Old Testament, including Malachi, points to Jesus. Christians are also supposed to point to Jesus. Circle boxes below that describe ways you can point to Christ.

SHARE THE GOSPEL WITH A FRIEND

GIVE MONEY TO MISSIONS

PLAY VIDEO GAMES ALL DAY

MAKE FUN OF SOMEONE AT SCHOOL

SERVE SOMEONE IN THE NAME OF CHRIST

INVITE SOMEONE TO CHURCH

USE MONEY ONLY ON YOURSELF

PRAY FOR PEOPLE

KEEP QUIET ABOUT JESUS SO TO NOT UPSET ANYONE

Which of these is the easiest for you? The hardest? Take a moment to pray that God will enable you to grow in that area.

TRUSTING GOD'S POWER

Place this activity sheet on the ground and stand over it with a penny. Drop the penny from the height of your nose and try to land it perfectly in the circle below. Try five times and see what happens.

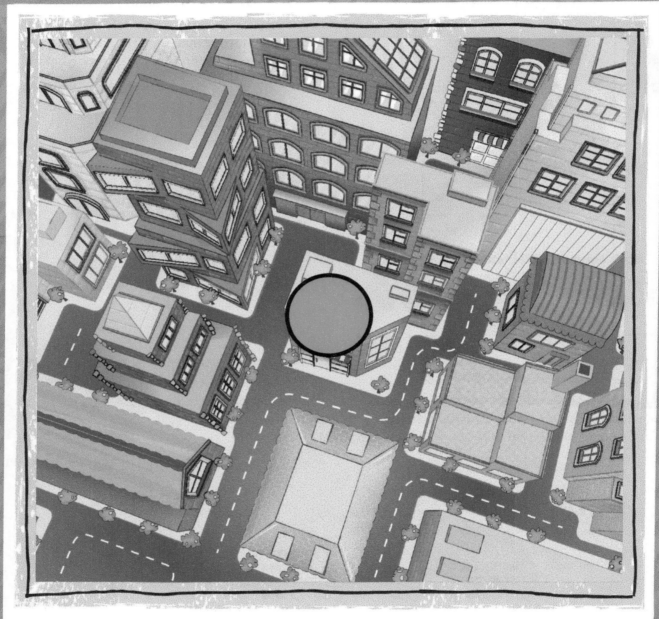

How'd you do? You likely didn't hit the circle perfectly once, let alone all five tries. Malachi predicted John the Baptist and the arrival of Jesus more than 400 years before they were born. Jesus also fulfilled hundreds of other prophecies in the Old Testament. For anyone other than God, this would be as difficult as standing on the top of an actual skyscraper, dropping a penny, and hitting the circle perfectly! The fulfilled promises of God prove that He's in control and can be trusted.

MANY NAMES

Use Isaiah 9:6 to find different names for Jesus. Then use these names to fill in the blanks and discover the secret message.

5.

1.

2.

3.

4.

1. _____ Father

2. Wonderful _____

3. _____ of Peace

4. _____ God

5. Another name for Jesus is

_____.

PRAYER PRACTICE

Jesus' mother Mary prayed to God for help. Read each Bible verse to discover a type of prayer you can pray. Write the kind of prayer in the box.

Psalm 95:2

I CAN PRAY A PRAYER OF ▶▶

Exodus 15:11

I CAN PRAY A PRAYER OF ▶▶

Mark 11:25

I CAN PRAY A PRAYER OF ▶▶

Psalm 6:4

I CAN PRAY A PRAYER OF ▶▶

James 5:16

I CAN PRAY A PRAYER OF ▶▶

MANY NAMES

Circle the correct word in the following sentences. Use your Bible to help you!

1. It is easier for a **LLAMA** **CAMEL** to go through the eye of a needle than for a rich person to enter the kingdom of God. (Mark 10:25)

2. He replied, "What is impossible with **MAN** **DOGS** is possible with God." (Luke 18:27)

3. I am able to do all things through him who **WEAKENS** **STRENGTHENS** me. (Philippians 4:13)

4. For nothing will be **IMPOSSIBLE** **POSSIBLE** with God. (Luke 1:37)

5. "For truly I tell you, if you have faith the size of a **MUSTARD** **WATERMELON** seed, you will tell this mountain, 'Move from here to there,' and it will move. Nothing will be impossible for you." (Matthew 17:20)

TILT-A-WORD

Tilt the page a little and look at the lines until you can see the letters. Read the word and fill in the first blank. Then turn the page until you are looking at it from the right side. Read the word and fill in the blank.

>> [_____] **WILL BE**

>> [_____] **WITH GOD!!**

LOST LEAVES

Match the leaf shapes to the blank leaves, then read the message about why Jesus came to earth.

save

seek

came

lost

Jesus

to

and

the

SHOW LOVE

Zacchaeus was not popular in his community, but Jesus still loved him. On the blank lines, write down a way you can show God's love to each person.

PEOPLE FROM OTHER COUNTRIES

THE HOMELESS

GRANDPARENTS

NEIGHBORS

NEW STUDENTS AT SCHOOL

PARENTS

SYMBOL OF SALVATION

	1	2	3	4	5	6	7	8	9
A	•	•	•	•	•	•	•	•	•
B	•	•	•	•	•	•	•	•	•
C	•	•	•	•	•	•	•	•	•
D	•	•	•	•	•	•	•	•	•
E	•	•	•	•	•	•	•	•	•
F	•	•	•	•	•	•	•	•	•
G	•	•	•	•	•	•	•	•	•
H	•	•	•	•	•	•	•	•	•
I	•	•	•	•	•	•	•	•	•
J	•	•	•	•	•	•	•	•	•
K	•	•	•	•	•	•	•	•	•

Color in each square from the grid code to
see a symbol of Jesus' love for us.

**A5 D1 K5 D7 D3 C5 I5 D6 D2 B5
J5 D9 H5 D4 G5 D8 F5 E5 D5**

SHOW YOU CARE

Jesus showed He cares for us by dying for our sins. You can show others you care for them, too! Draw a line from the picture to the ways you can show someone you care. There is more than one answer for each photo!

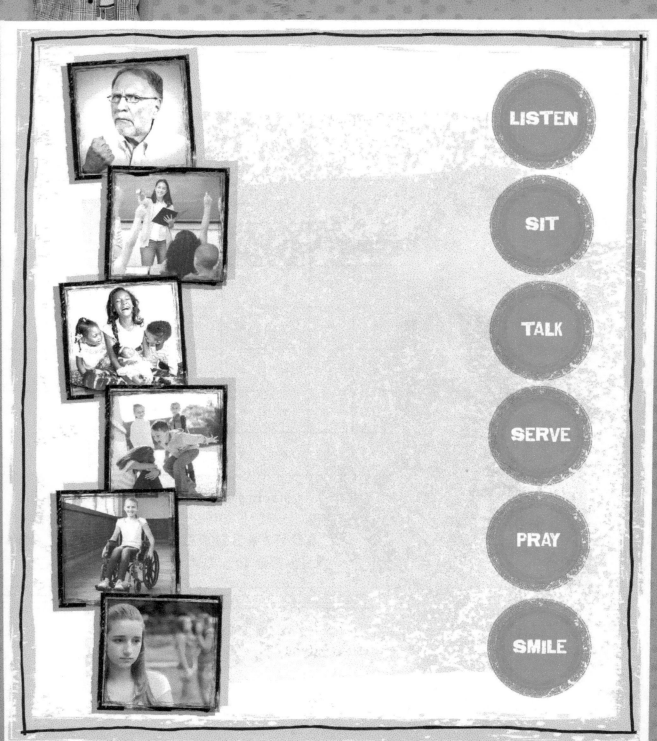

LISTEN

SIT

TALK

SERVE

PRAY

SMILE

HIDDEN MESSAGE

Hidden among the different symbols are letters. Circle each letter to fill in the blanks to find out what Peter's vision meant.

)&$G}\(^&*$&*$%#o$#&d('&($s(*)(#!

__ __ __ __ '__

}*)(*&%W&*{|o)(*&r@!<d(*^$(s&(#^#

__ __ __ __ __

^%$i}&${%@|(]])#(°&^%$#:=!s#%@)@

__ __

@!<?(*^f(*&(#%@o|#(°&(({]r[))(^%$#@

__ __ __

&*e$%#$^v]=?@e$!r{@&y> o&#n?>e

__ __ __ __ __ __ __ __

GOLDFISH GOBBLE

Sometimes following God's Word isn't easy. Use the goldfish key to help you decide how many goldfish to shade in as your response to each situation.

 EASY   **A LITTLE HARDER**   **VERY HARD**

Tell a friend about Jesus.

Invite a classmate to a church activity.

Be nice to a new visitor at church.

Share a verse with a friend who doesn't go to church.

PICTURE PERFECT

Number the pictures in the order that they happened in the story of Paul and Silas in prison.

SHARING SALVATION

God's followers share their faith with others just like Paul and Silas. Fill in the blanks of the following verses. Put a star next to the ones you use to tell others about Jesus!

SAVED   GOD   SAVED   POWER   EVERYONE

SALVATION   CONFESS   BELIEVE   GOSPEL   SALVATION

BELIEVE   NAME   SAVED

1. *Acts 16:31* " _____ in the Lord Jesus, and you will be _____ ."

2. *Romans 10:9* If you _____ with your mouth, "Jesus is Lord," and _____ in your heart that God raised him from the dead, you will be _____ .

3. *Acts 4:12* There is _____ in no one else, for there is no other _____ under heaven given to people by which we must be _____ .

4. *Psalm 62:1* I am at rest in _____ alone; my _____ comes from him.

5. *Romans 1:16* For I am not ashamed of the _____ , because it is the _____ of God for salvation to _____ who believes.

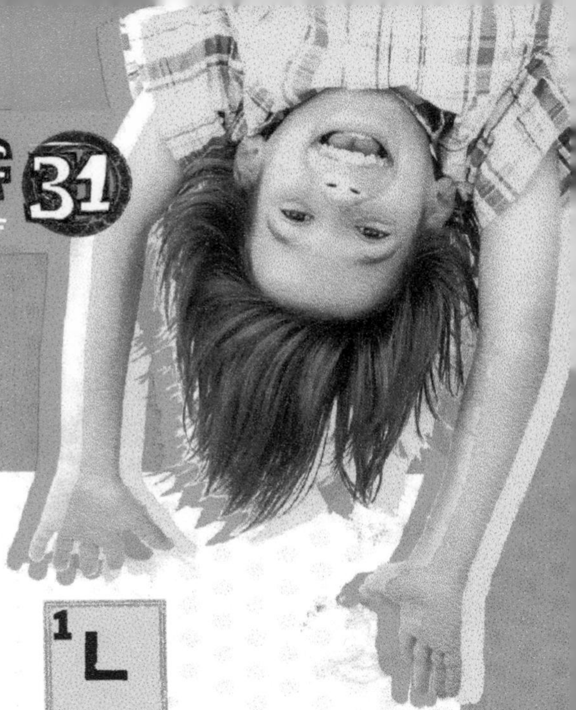

FILL IT IN

Put each word from today's story from the box in the correct space. The first letter of each word is there to help you!

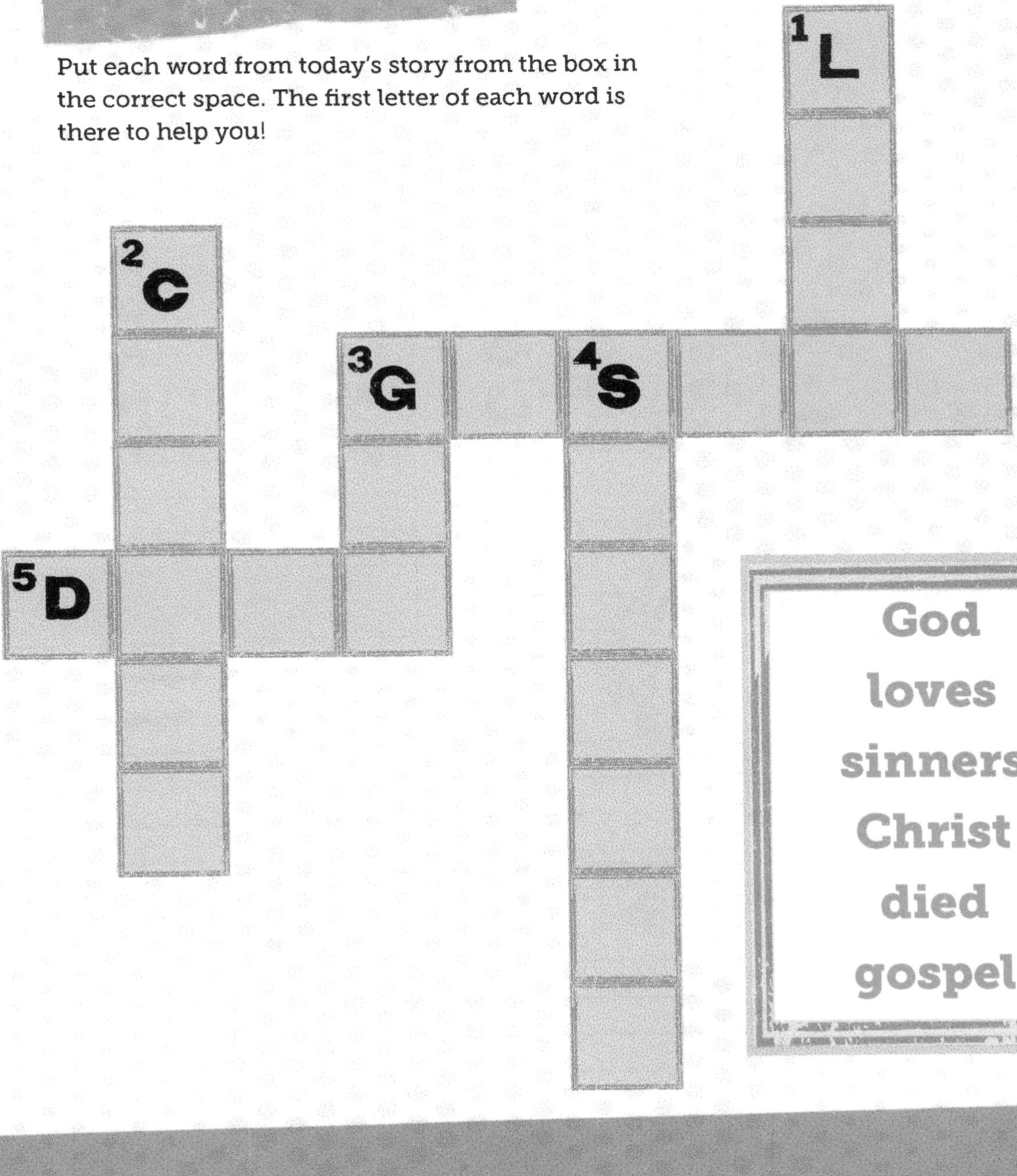

¹L

²C

³G   ⁴S

⁵D

God

loves

sinners

Christ

died

gospel

SPECIAL ACCESS

Ephesians 2:18 tells us we have access to someone special because of Jesus. Use the code to find out who helps us!

A=   D=   C=
E=   N=   R=
I=   P=   G=
O=   L=   S=
U=   W=   H=
Y=   V=   T=

PHRASE PUZZLE

Using the colored blocks to guide you, put each piece of the puzzle in the correct spot to read today's memory verse.

Using the pictures as clues, unscramble each word below. Then circle the things that God is in charge of.

H S O C O L

_ _ _ _ _ _

D W L O R

_ _ _ _ _

A M F Y I L

_ _ _ _ _ _

E E W T A H R

_ _ _ _ _ _ _

S D F I N R E

_ _ _ _ _ _ _

that lies

the race

before us.

Let us

endurance

run with

A-MAZE-ING FAITH

Find the words from today's verse in the maze. Then write the verse in order below.

REJOICE!!

James 1:2 tells believers to be joyful during hard times. Read the situations below and write ways you can praise God during each of them.

A PET DIED

»
_____
_____
_____
_____
_____

GOT IN TROUBLE AT SCHOOL

»
_____
_____
_____
_____
_____
_____

MADE A BAD GRADE

»
_____
_____
_____
_____

LOST A SPORTS GAME

»
_____
_____
_____
_____
_____

FRIENDS MADE FUN OF YOU

»
_____
_____
_____
_____
_____

PARENTS FIGHTING

»
_____
_____
_____
_____

SHOWING FAITH

Use the code key to find out how to show others your faith in God.

A= ↺ N= C
B= ↑ O= ↔
D= ↶ R= ↗
E= ▶▶ S= ←
F= ⋘ T= ⋀
H= ⊙ W= ↖
J= ↗ Y= ↜
L= ⬆ 1= ◀
M= ✓ 2= ◁

GOOD WORKS

Doing good works is how others know we love Jesus. Read the situations below, and circle the ones that show good works.

Julie reads her Bible a little every day.

Alec uses swear words.

Carter stopped hanging out with trouble-making friends.

Eva tattles to get her sister in trouble.

Jace turns off TV shows with bad language.

Josie says she did her homework when she didn't.

PUZZLING WORDS

Solve the word puzzle to find out what Christians are called to be in Ephesians 4:4.

 - HY

B + [SODA] - SA + Y

___ ___ ___

___ ___ ___

>> USE YOUR BODY

Just like your body parts have special jobs, each part of the Body of Christ can serve in special ways. Draw lines from examples of serving to the matching body part.

>> **Listen to the preacher's sermons.**

>> **Watch the babies in the nursery on Sunday mornings.**

>> **Sing praise songs in the children's choir.**

>> **Go with other church members to tell people about Jesus.**

>> **Pack boxes of food or toys for people in need.**

SPECIAL LETTERS

Isaiah 25:8 tells us a wonderful truth about life in heaven. Use the letter clues to find out what will be gone in heaven!

THE LETTER BEFORE E ◯

THE ONLY VOWEL IN THE WORD "LETTER" ◯

THE FIRST LETTER OF THE ALPHABET ◯

THE LETTER THE CROSS MAKES ◯

THE LETTER AFTER G ◯

AS IT IS IN HEAVEN

Things will be very different in heaven than they are on earth! Cross out the words of things that won't be in heaven. Circle the things that will be in heaven. Use today's passage in Revelation 21:1-4, 22-27 to help you!

SUN

PAIN

SEA

CRYING

THRONE

MOON

HOLY CITY

JESUS

Dear Parents,

We thank you for giving us the opportunity to work with your child in TeamKID. TeamKID is a fun, high-energy ministry that encourages kids to know Jesus Christ and to grow in a relationship with Him. All parts of TeamKID — Bible stories, Bible verses, life application, missions, and recreation — connect to teach life lessons to kids.

The TeamKID motto is descriptive of what we try to accomplish in the club:

- Learning About God
- Using the Bible
- Living for Jesus

TeamKID helps children through a study of God's Word. Using fun activities and Bible material, children can apply the Bible verses they learn to know how God wants them to live. A missions feature every week will open their eyes to the need of people around the world to hear about Jesus.

On the opposite side of this letter you will find a list of the topics we will be studying. We pray God will use these resources and our teaching to help your children apply these messages to their lives.

Sincerely,

The TeamKID Team

TOPICS YOUR CHILDREN WILL BE STUDYING IN TEAMKID

1 ☐ God Created

2 ☐ God Calls a People of Faith

3 ☐ God Delivers His People

4 ☐ God Offers Atonement

5 ☐ God Provides a Substitute

6 ☐ God Requires Righteousness

7 ☐ God Provides a Place for His People

8 ☐ God Provides Salvation

9 ☐ God Redeems His People

10 ☐ God Provides a King

11 ☐ God's Kings Reject Him

12 ☐ God Builds a Kingdom

13 ☐ God Uses Suffering

14 ☐ God Divides the Righteous & Wicked

15 ☐ God's People Seek Wisdom

16 ☐ God Rebuilds the Broken

17 ☐ God's People Work Together on Mission

18 ☐ God Saves His People

19 ☐ God Has a Plan

20 ☐ God's New Covenant

21 ☐ God Shepherds His People

22 ☐ God Trains Faithful Exiles

23 ☐ God's Great Mercy

24 ☐ God Prepares the Way

25 ☐ God Becomes a Man

26 ☐ God Does the Impossible

27 ☐ God Requires Repentance

28 ☐ God Died and Rose for Sinners

29 ☐ God's Gospel Is for Everyone

30 ☐ God's Followers Share Their Faith

31 ☐ God Reconciles Sinners to Himself

32 ☐ God Is Above All

33 ☐ God Is the Perfecter of Faith

34 ☐ God Creates Fruit in His Followers

35 ☐ God's People Love Differently

36 ☐ God Plans the Future

GOD LOVES YOUR FAMILY

In the frame below, draw a picture of your family. Tell them about the things you are learning in TeamKID!